RULES TO THIS ISH-UNEDITED
BY GEARY DAVIS

ISBN 978-1-9991088-0-9

"Envision Big Things"

This isn't the same thing as "dreaming big." Dreams are usually twisted fantasies of reality. Envisioning is a matter of reality.

"Don't be afraid to be judged."

The fear that most people have about starting their own business, is the fear of judgment. People can't love your product, if they don't have the ability to hate it.

"When spending money, think business first."

Some people love to shop. I advise those people to look at business expenses as shopping. Find pleasure in buying for your business.

"Find inspiration from things that are not related to what you're doing."

I look for my business inspiration from companies and organizations that are completely different from what I'm doing. That normally drives creativity.

"Never speak of yourself in the future tense."

If you believe that "one day" you'll be successful, you're right. It's just not today, or tomorrow. Speak it now.

"Study criminals."

Most successful families have a criminal past. Study that past to learn how they transitioned from illegal to legal. Criminals are often very business savvy.

"Understand why broke people, are broke."

There's a big difference between broke and poor. If you're living in the United States, Canada, Germany   etc, chances are you're just broke. Poor people have nothing, broke people have things that they can't pay for. There's power in understanding how people think.

"Embrace embarrassment"

Just as you have to OK with being judged, you have to become comfortable with embarrassment. What you'll find is that over time, what embarrasses you, no longer will. That's when you're comfortable in your own skin.

"Be willing to sacrifice credit now, for wealth later"

If an entrepreneur is faced with the choice between paying a bill, or making a good investment, good entrepreneurs will make the investment.

"Know the value of things"

We've all heard that there's a difference between cost and value. What we don't discuss is the personal value of things. If I need a particular screw to complete a multi-million dollar creation, that screw has lots of value to me. So much so, that I'd be willing to pay way more than it's worth to someone else.

"Know the value of people"

Just as things have different value according to who needs it, so do people. Everyone around you has some type of value in your life. Understand how to extract that value by adding value to them.

"Never use people"

Extracting value from people isn't the same thing as using them. Used people usually don't know that they're being used; whereas valuable people should always know their value to you.

"Don't expect anyone to be happy for you"

In spite of what you believe, people should not be happy for your success. It does nothing for them unless you bring value to their lives.

"Find reasons to pay other people"

Because most people will not be happy for your success, it's important to pay people whenever possible. If someone does something small for you, pay them something. That keeps their hatred at bay.

"If you can't pay people, find ways to help them make money"

Sometimes the best payment to someone, is in the form of opportunity.

"Befriend the bad guys"

There are always bad guys and gals around you, find a way to befriend them. In most cases, these people aren't friendly, however, they are human and have human needs. Watch for an opportunity to help fulfill their needs.

"Get to know the broke people around you"

In capitalism everyone wants to feel wealthy. For many people, shopping does it for them. Find out what these people are buying, and get them as customers. If they're going to waste their money, they can at least waste it on your business.

"Give back whenever possible"

This doesn't mean that you have to have millions of dollars. Giving back means that you sacrifice profit for human decency.

"Don't be ashamed of seeking profit"

Everyone is in business to make money, don't be ashamed of it. People respect you more when you're honest.

"Understand that people want to be sold on an idea"

If someone stops to look at your product or service, understand that they WANT to buy what you have. What they're looking for is a reason to buy. Give them a reason.

"Understand that some people look for reasons NOT to buy"

Just as there are people who are looking for reasons to buy your product, there are people who want to buy it, but their minds are trying to talk them out of it. You have to learn how to bypass their brains.

"Make your product or service, a need"

In order to bypass their brains, you have to learn how to embed your business into the "needs" section of their psyche. When people feel that they need something, it becomes a rational purchase.

"Make sure that you idea is a rational purchase"

People don't like to purchase irrational things. No one wants to buy a box of corn flakes for $500. That's completely irrational. However, someone would consider paying $500 for a box of corn flakes that was owned by a celebrity. There's a secret there.

"Be willing to be viewed as crazy"

Sometimes the best ideas are convoluted. There's this belief that an idea has to be simple, I call that nonsense. Some of the best ideas sound crazy at their creation. Try to imagine how crazy it would sound to explain Instagram to someone 30 years ago.

"Understand that there are codes to everything in life"

Because everything exists because of something else, it's important to understand origins. The origin of an idea usually contains the source code of success.

"Learn the pattern of success"

Just as there are codes, there are also patterns. Going from A to B to C, will lead you to D etc. Spend a respectable amount of time studying the pattern of success for your industry.

"Learn the pattern of failure"

Just as there are patterns for success, there are patterns for failure. When businesses fail, it's usually because of a particular set of reasons. Learn those reasons and avoid them.

"Embrace change"

Change doesn't happen in a vacuum. In most cases, change is the result of the masses choosing to adopt that change. Don't fight against the people.

"Understand that businesses set trends, not people"

You have the freedom of choice, but only between the choices that we give you. When you walk into a store, you can only buy what they sell. Use that knowledge to run your business accordingly.

"You can't completely buck trends, only adjust them"

Just as businesses set trends, very few business attempt to completely change them. Just look around you and you'll notice that products have changed, however their change was gradual. Never try to completely change a trend.

"It doesn't take money to make money"

If it takes money to makes money, how was the first money made? What it actually takes are products, customers, and a unit of account.

"Know that all businesses start small"

No big business began as one. Even Walmart began as a small store in the South. Big businesses are the result of combining a good idea, with lots of customers.

"Learn to see the future"

I have a habit of foreseeing the end of something, from the beginning. If I can't predict how bad or good something could end, I usually avoid it. That means that there is something that I'm missing.

"Factor in the things that you don't know"

You don't know exactly what you don't know, but you do know what you know. Examine what you know and find the unanswered questions.

"Understand that marketing is far more valuable than product"

People don't buy products, they buy marketing. Every product has weaknesses, however good companies make sure to sell the strengths.

"Focus on your strengths, not your
weaknesses"

No matter how hard you try, there will
always be things that you are weak at.
Don't waste your time on those. Just focus
on becoming extremely strong in your
strengths.

"Read lots of books"

Reading is a really good way of expanding your understanding about life. The more you understand about life, the better ideas you can generate.

"Own your ideas, even if you don't plan to execute them"

There have been plenty of ideas that I've chosen not to pursue, however I still bought domain names, copyrights etc. Just in case.

"Sell any unused ideas you have"

If I come up with an idea that I don't plan
to use, I find someone who can execute it,
and I sell it to them by helping them
launch their business.

"Get involved in helping others start their business"

Don't be afraid to help others get their ideas off of the ground. Helping others in their business, could help you get ideas for your own.

"Never give away anything for free, except your time"

Once you start giving away products, it becomes very difficult to start charging a fee for it. You can start cheaper, then increase your prices, but never go for free. It is, however, OK to give away some of your time to help others.

"Remember that cheaper is fine, but cheap never is"

You can offer your products and services for a lower price, but it's never a good idea to be the cheapest. When you're the cheapest, people devalue your business in their minds.

"The perception of your business is more valuable than the reality"

This goes without explanation.

"Never attempt to explain your failures"

If you're having a conversation about losses, it's a losing conversation. Failure are irrelevant.

"Keep conversations short"

The fewer words you speak, the more valuable they are once they're spoken. Learn how to shut up.

"Listen with your eyes"

People say one thing, but do another. Rarely believe what you hear, and always believe what you see.

"Feel with your gut"

There's a theory out that claims that your intestines, are in fact, a second brain. If something doesn't feel right, don't do it.

"Form conclusions quickly, but act on them slowly"

Observe the world around you, and form a base understanding. Once you've done that, slowly begin to run thoughts through that understanding. Only when a thought as pass that test, should it be acted upon.

"Learn to really listen to music"

Have you ever sang the words to a song, just to realize that you never listen to the lyrics? There are lots of thoughts expressed through music, learn to listen to those thoughts.

"You can never succeed beyond your thoughts"

You have to think of your business in the largest idea. How big or small you envision your business, sets your realistic boundaries.

"Never nationalize your ideas"

I never have an American or Canadian idea. I try to create ideas that would work in at least a dozen countries.

"Learn a new language"

The beauty of learning a new language is that it allows you to communicate with people from other cultures. That enable you to make connections that you wouldn't have been able to make otherwise.

"Make cross-cultural connections"

Connecting with people from other cultures allows you to see the world from a different perspective. Having different perspectives gives you an upper edge in business.

"Understand that business is always personal"

Business success relies on other people's money, and there's nothing more personal than that. People work hard for their money, so patronizing your business is a very personal matter.

"Keep your personal feelings out of business"

Although business is extremely personal, it should never be so to the owner of the business. As a business owner, your primary goal is to make money. Always respect your customers.

"Respect your future competition"

Even if you are great at what you do, always understand that competition will arise. Wherever there is success, competition will flock there.

"It's OK to quit"

Life is measured out to every individual in unequal measures. Don't waste your time doing something that isn't making you happy.

"Business doesn't have to make you happy, it just can't make you unhappy"

You don't have to love what you do, just don't hate it. I don't particularly love fast food, but I'd have no problem owning a burger joint, if it made sense.

"Minimize your overhead"

If you DO decide to open a burger joint, it's going to be a very expensive endeavor to start. I try to avoid starting any business that requires more than $1,000 in start up capital.

"Never risk more than you can afford to lose"

This is why I don't believe in getting loans to start businesses. If you can't afford to finance the business, you could never afford to lose the business. The last thing you want is to start a failed business, just to end up in debt.

"Only enter into business deals with other businesses"

It may seem like a good idea to have employees, but I've learned that contracting other businesses is a much better idea. You want to deal with people who think the same as you. Employees see the world differently than employers.

"Learn to sell people on a way of thinking"

When it comes to being an entrepreneur, it's important to sell people on how you think, not the idea itself. Entrepreneurs are a different breed than most. We tend to see the world as opportunities, not success and failures.

"Learn to see opportunities"

I've done everything from selling food items, to MLM. I didn't care about whether or not I was the right person to execute the idea, I only cared about the viability of the idea.

"Never allow your personality to dictate your ideas"

A lot of people are afraid to start certain types of businesses because it doesn't fit their personality. Just remember that you are the owner of the business, not the manager. Leave the personality stuff to your hired management team.

"Remember that all businesses are ran the same"

It doesn't matter what type of business you're stating, they're all managed using the same math. The X's and O's are the same. Don't get intimidated by the little things.

"Understand that no business is bigger than you"

Every year there are multiple businesses that close their doors for good. Just remember that closing a business doesn't change who you are as a person.

"Always control the narrative"

There's a reason why large companies hire PR firms. You want to be able to control your own press. Write articles, blogs etc that explain your business actions. Don't allow others to define you.

"Understand that there are no good or bad people"

Everyone is capable of doing both good and bad, and the idea of good and bad are subjective. When it comes to business, you sometimes have to do things that will cause people to question you as a person. As long as you are causing the least amount of damage, you should sleep well.

"Remember that creation is also the act of destruction"

When you're perusing a business idea, remember that your success will be someone else's failure. That's an immutable fact.

"Minimize your risk"

Entrepreneurs are not risk takers. We are analytically inclined thinkers, who identify opportunity for commerce.

"Know that capitalism is only designed to grow businesses"

Employees will always get screwed over in a capitalist society because the laws are designed for corporate incubation. That's why it's important to own your own business.

"Understand that the middle class doesn't exist"

There is no such thing as a middle class. What we have is a transitional class. Middle class people will either become rich or poor. Nothing in between.

"Know that paychecks will eventually go away, but wealth won't"

As the middle class ceases to exist, incomes will follow. We're not seeing the disappearance of cash, we're witnessing the disappearance of money. The things that you own are extremely important.

"Keep most of your wealth in assets, and the rest in cash"

Starting and running businesses is the best place to spend your money. The more businesses you own, the more opportunities you have to earn cash. There will come a point in time when cards won't work, so keep some cash handy.

"Digitize your business as much as possible, but keep the most important aspects tangible"

Just because your business is online, it doesn't mean that it all has to be. The human side of your business is the most important aspect of your business, so never try to digitize or automate it. Keep it physical.

"Create experiences, not products"

Keeping in line with not digitizing the human element of your business, it's also important to cater to the human element. We love great experiences, so keep that as an important part of your business.

"Price your work according to value"

I understand the value that I bring to the table, so I make sure to price my work according to the information that I'm giving. You should do the same.

"Adjust your life to appreciate value"

Get rid of all of the things that don't have any real value in your life. Whatever doesn't give value, is taking away value.

"Shop from yourself"

If you wouldn't shop from you, why would someone else? Create "you" quality products.

"Support like businesses"

Supporting like businesses will ensure the survival of your industry. If you are the only product in your space, then your space doesn't exist.

"Seek opportunities to combine industries"

I try to always find ways to combine industries. If you want to do something fun, try to find a way to combine real estate and literature. The innovator thinkers will find a way.

"Become comfortable being alone"

Sometimes innovation and creation are lonely processes. You have to become completely comfortable with being alone with your thoughts.

"Learn to decipher which thoughts are yours, and which are implanted by others"

People have the ability to download thoughts into your mind by giving you their psychological baggage. When people are sharing their negative thoughts with you, they are actually transferring those thoughts over to you. Examine the source of your thoughts.

"Be aware that some people are trading thoughts with you"

As people pass their negative thoughts off to you, they're soliciting positive thoughts from you. The more you share positive thoughts with negative people, the more you'll notice that your thoughts will become more negative. They've essentially traded thoughts with you.

"Avoid people who lack vision"

As an entrepreneur you will become used to living a life that's guided by visions of things better. When you are around people who lack vision, their energy will cause you to lose focus on your own.

"Every idea is rooted in an energy, don't waste it"

If you've ever tried to explain a great idea to someone who doesn't get it, you know the feeling of lack that follows. When you speak of an idea to someone, you're giving that person the authority to either validate, or invalidate your idea. Don't waste your time.

"Don't waste words"

Actions are far more valuable than words, so focus on actions. The more you talk, the harder it becomes to put those words into action. Only speak when necessary.

"Don't waste time"

Wasting time is done when you are not working towards your goals. Even if we are doing things that make us happy, if they're not moving us towards our goals, they're nothing more than distractions.

"Remember that life is to be lived, not necessarily enjoyed"

There's a reason why you're still breathing, and it's not because you need to have more fun. Get to work.

"Understand that working is a part of life"

We often hear people say that they'll retire and start living. That's the wrong mentality. The reality is that working is a part of living, the problem is that they're doing the wrong type of work.

"If you HAVE to work a job, do something that you would do off of the clock"

Never work a job that you hate. Hatred is nothing more than the energy of destruction, so you're essentially destroying yourself for 8 hours a day.

"Streamline your own production process"

Once you're in the habit of executing your ideas, create a process that expedites the process. Figure out where you waste the most time in getting started, and work to improve it. Your mind is the "home office" to all of your ideas. Keep it organized.

"Don't waste time thinking about people who aren't paying you"

If someone isn't paying you to think about them, don't. Negative people do not deserve your energy.

"Hire your friends to do small tasks for you"

You would be surprised at how talented your friends are. Find ways to contract their intelligence. This keeps them happy and out of your way.

"Bring your family along for the ride"

Your partner/spouse may not always support what you're doing, but it doesn't hurt to keep them in the loop. There may come a point in time when they accept your reality, and offer valuable input.

"Listen to criticism"

No one thinks their children are ugly, but some may be. There are times when you need to hear the truth.

"Stay above the law"

The fastest way to end your business is to not cooperate with all of the legal requirements of owning a business. Make sure that you work with the law at all times.

"Find the right country for your business"

I've come to learn that some of my businesses are uniquely Canadian, whereas some are American. I didn't plan it that way, but it's the truth.

"Embrace your real customers"

You can never predict who will gravitate to your business, but when you find out who they are, accept it. Don't kill your idea because your customers are different than you.

"Remember that you're always going to be a student"

There is no mastery of knowledge on this planet, so none of us can claim to be teachers. I only know how to share the information that I've learned, but I know that I'm still learning.

"Avoid doing business with conspiracy theorists"

Now I enjoy a good conspiracy just as much as the next person, but I've noticed that many conspiracy theorists talk themselves out of making good investments. They never have any proof of what they believe, they just know that it's bad. Avoid that negative energy.

"Learn the ins and outs of banking"

I'm a cash guy, so I try to keep my banking interactions to a minimum. I will, however, admit that the banking system is fascinating. The way in which they set traps for people, is a thing of beauty. You should know how they work.

"Understand that there are 2 economies; the one that the average person sees, and the one that's only visible to the wealthy"

Credit scores are for poor people who seek access to wealthy people's money. When rich people seek financing to expand a business, they don't have to apply for business loans; they partner with a financing entity. You real credit is your ability to create a profitable business entity.

"Turn yourself into a business"

The phrase "game recognizes game" applies ever-so-deeply to business. Always conduct yourself as a business entity because businesses demand higher respect. It's much easier to get someone to partner with you as a business, than as an individual.

"Learn old business models"

Sometimes doing things differently, means doing them the old way. As business processes evolve, they tend to leave behind a trail of defunct business models. If you're able to amply learn and apply these models, you could oddly be seen as an innovator. There's always going to be a market for the old ways.

"Don't seek to gain customers, seek to exclude them"

You should only want customers who really want you. We've all heard the stories of the recording artist who sold millions of albums, just to fall off and only sell a few thousand years later. The reality is that those few thousand customers are their real fans. Knowing your true number of customers, enables you to build a solid base for your business. You want to get rid of the people who are bandwagon supporters.

"Understand that most people are followers, so give them something to follow"

In many situations, people only buy what other people are buying around them. Just look at the iPhone as an example. I think they are terrible phones, but people buy them out of fear. They are afraid to NOT have the latest gadget. You have to think the same way for your business. Focus on tagging your product to an existing idea.

"If you can't create an original idea, focus on creating an accessory to an existing one"

There are tons of opportunities around you, you just have to look for them. Just think about everything that you own, I'm sure there are dozens of opportunities to improve upon some of those ideas. In many cases, all it would take is an engineering drawing and a patent.

"If you can't finance an idea, seek to sell it"

Going back to the previous rule, if you can get the legal rights to an idea, you can take your idea to potential buyers. You'd be surprised at how easy it is to get meetings with big companies. In many situations, all it takes is an email. Don't be afraid to sell enough ideas to raise enough capital to finance your own.

"See through the illusion of the world"

The world around you is nothing more than an illusion. What appears to be ownership is nothing more than debt. Owning the things in your life, should be more important than appearing to be wealthy. Get to know what it really takes to be free.

"Know that sometimes, education can hinder the entrepreneurial spirit"

The modern educational system was designed to create employees, not bosses. The amount of time and money people invest into education, can sometimes make them disillusioned about it's value. The reality is that a large number of the world's greatest entrepreneurs have either dropped out of college, or have never gone. Creativity doesn't need permission to exist.

"Understand that freedom is expensive, but it doesn't cost a lot of money"

The amount of mental energy required to become a successful entrepreneur, is what makes it expensive. You have to force yourself to think about your endeavors, more than you would like.

"Have long conversations with yourself"

Because the mind is the source of all ideas, it's important that you spend a lot of time with yours. Find that quiet place that allows you to converse with every idea that enters your mind. That's the only way to understand their potential.

END OF THIS VOLUME